# NATIONS IN CONFLICT

# IRAQ

## by PEGGY J. PARKS

**BLACKBIRCH®**
**PRESS**

**THOMSON**
**GALE**

San Diego • Detroit • New York • San Francisco • Cleveland • New Haven, Conn. • Waterville, Maine • London • Munich

Photo credits: cover, pages 4, 6-7, 11, 15, 16, 21, 25, 30, 31, 33, 34, 40, 41, 43 © CORBIS; page 5 (map) Amy Stirnkorb Design; pages 8, 9, 36-37, 39 © AP Wide World; pages 12, 27, 29 © Corel Corporation; page 13 © Getty Images; page 17 © Art Resource; pages 19, 22 © Hulton Archive

**LIBRARY OF CONGRESS CATALOGING-IN-PUBLICATION DATA**

Parks, Peggy J., 1951-
  Iraq / by Peggy J. Parks.
    v. cm. — (Nations in conflict series)
  Includes bibliographical references and index.
  Contents: Place, people, past — Political turmoil — An uncertain
future.
  ISBN 1-41030-078-1 (lib. : alk. paper)
  1. Iraq—Juvenile literature. [1. Iraq.] I. Title. II. Series.

DS70.62 .P37 2003
956.7—dc21                                                2002015884

Printed in United States
10 9 8 7 6 5 4 3 2 1

# CONTENTS

# A Troubled Nation

Iraq is a country that has long been in a state of uncertainty and turmoil. This is largely due to its oppressive government, which was taken over by Saddam Hussein in 1979. Hussein quickly proved to be one of the most brutal leaders in history. Sandra Mackey, an author and freelance journalist who lived in Iraq, described his effect on the people: "For Iraqis trapped in the fear and brutality of Hussein's [dictatorship], ordinary life is a deadly serious game. Spies lurk everywhere, ready to turn the most casual comment into grounds for imprisonment or execution. Engulfed in this cocoon of fear, people keep to themselves. This isolation of Iraqis from foreigners and from each other has totally changed the atmosphere of Iraq. ... Now, a current of tension runs through every encounter with an Iraqi."[1]

Saddam Hussein took office as president of Iraq in 1979 and assumed tyrannical control of the country.

The Hussein regime caused years of hardship for Iraq and its
people. The country was devastated by two wars, the first of which
was a bloody eight-year conflict with Iran. The second was the Persian
Gulf War, fought against the United States and a coalition, or unified

group, of countries that protested Iraq's invasion of Kuwait. Those wars left Iraq burdened with billions of dollars in war debt, as well as country-wide destruction. Hundreds of thousands of Iraqis were killed or injured, and many others fled Iraq to seek refuge in neighboring countries. Iraq's wars also severely damaged the nation's infrastructure—its transportation and communication systems and its water, sewage, and electrical power systems. This caused the country's drinking water to become contaminated, which contributed to a rapid spread of infectious diseases, especially among Iraq's children. United Nations (UN) sanctions, which were intended to force Hussein to give up weapons of mass destruction, contributed to shortages of food and medical supplies.

Two wars since 1979 have destroyed buildings throughout Iraq.

With water systems damaged by war, Iraqis must carry water from rivers to their homes.

Mackey, who lived in Saudi Arabia for about ten years, first visited Iraq in the 1970s. When she returned twenty years later, she was shocked at how the country had changed. She explains: "I stepped into Iraq in 1998 to find the country a ghost of the Iraq of the late 1970s. The Iraqis had been devastated by two wars. ... Across the city, the shelves of stores that had once bulged with imported goods from the United States, Europe, and Asia were almost empty. The educational system that had promised to educate every child and to train the finest doctors, engineers, and scholars was in shambles. ... But more than anything, Iraq had become a prison in which everyone lived in fear of its warden—Saddam Hussein."[2]

In March 2003, a U.S.-led coalition began to bomb targeted locations throughout Iraq. The goal, as stated by U.S. president George W. Bush, was "to disarm Iraq, to free its people, and to defend the world from grave danger."[3] He believed that there was only one way to achieve that goal—and that was to rid the world of Saddam Hussein.

**Opposite page:** With much of the population starving, some Iraqis are forced to search through garbage dumps for food.

# CHAPTER ONE

# Place, People, Past

Iraq is part of a cluster of countries known as the Middle East, located on the southwest side of the Asian continent. With an area of about 169,000 square miles, the nation is a bit larger than the state of California. In ancient times, present-day Iraq was called Mesopotamia, a Greek word that means "the land between the rivers." These rivers are the Tigris and Euphrates, which run through Iraq from north to south and surround the capital city of Baghdad.

Iraq is bordered on the south by Kuwait, the Persian Gulf, and Saudi Arabia. To the north is Turkey, and to the west are Jordan and Syria. Iran lies to the east. Fertile lowlands make up the central part of Iraq, and the Syrian Desert covers the south. These different

**Left:** The Euphrates River runs through Iraq from north to south.

**Right:** Because much of Iraq is desert, most crops are grown in very dry soil.

Pumping stations draw oil from the ground. Oil is Iraq's most valuable resource.

regions often experience extreme climates. Some of the hottest temperatures in the world have been recorded in southern Iraq, and severe dust storms and sandstorms are common in the desert. In the mountains, however, summers are short and winters are very cold.

## Abundant Natural Resources

In the central area of Iraq, near the Tigris and Euphrates rivers, there is rich farmland. The country receives scant rainfall—usually no more than ten inches per year—but water from the rivers provides irrigation for crops. Some of the main crops grown are wheat, barley, and rice. Other major crops include cotton and dates. In fact, Iraqi dates have long been known as some of the finest in the world. Although many date palm trees were damaged or destroyed through years of war, the country is still one of the largest date producers in the world.

Although agriculture is important to Iraq, the country's most valuable resources lie beneath the surface of the earth. Vast quantities of oil and natural gas are found in the south, near the Persian Gulf, as well as in the north and northeast. With an estimated 112 billion barrels of oil, Iraq holds about 11 percent of the total oil reserves in the world—second only to Saudi Arabia. In addition, Iraq has 110 trillion cubic feet of natural gas. Iraq's export of oil and natural gas has traditionally accounted for about 95 percent of the country's income. Despite their great potential wealth, however, the nation's many resources benefit just a small percentage of Iraq's diverse population.

## The People of Iraq

About 23 million people live in Iraq. More than three-fourths of them are Arabian, and Arabic is the nation's primary language. There are also several ethnic minorities, including Turkomans, Assyrians, and Marsh Arabs, or Ma'dan.

The Kurds are another ethnic group, and they make up about 20 percent of the population. Kurdish people have their own

Women pray at a mosque in Baghdad. The vast majority of Iraqis are Muslim.

# MARSH ARABS: LIVING REMNANTS OF AN ANCIENT SOCIETY

**Marsh Arabs, also called Ma'dan, are descendants of the ancient Sumerians and Babylonians.** For thousands of years, these people have dwelled in the marshy areas that were once part of Mesopotamia and are now part of Iraq. Many believe that the Ma'dan are modern members of the oldest living civilization in the world. Throughout history, the Ma'dan have maintained their separate culture and ancient traditions. They have continued to thrive, protected by the wilderness of the marshes.

Since Sumerian times, the lives of the Ma'dan have revolved around water. They raise water buffalo and hunt and fish in the marshes. They also farm and grow rice. They depend heavily on reed, a form of tall grass that is abundant in wetland areas. The Ma'dan use reed to build canoe-like boats and huge, cathedral-style homes.

They also weave mats from reed. They even live on islands that are constructed entirely of reed.

The marshes where the Ma'dan have survived for centuries were once the largest wetland system in the Middle East and covered nearly 8,000 square miles. Today, however, 90 percent of those wetlands have disappeared because the Iraqi government has drained them. The government says it has done this because the Ma'dan allow criminals to hide in the marshes. It is widely believed, however, that Saddam Hussein's real motive is to get rid of the Ma'dan entirely.

When the wetlands are drained, an area where lush vegetation and wildlife have grown for hundreds of years is left dry, barren, and salt-encrusted. As the wetlands have dried up, the ancient Ma'dan population has dwindled from more than half a

**Marsh Arabs live in villages built on water.**

million in 1980 to barely thirty thousand today.

Thousands of the Ma'dan who lost their homes in Iraq's wetlands have fled to refugee camps in neighboring Iran. Others have moved to different parts of Iraq, where they have tried to start new lives. The few Ma'dan who remain in Iraq's wetlands still survive—but as the wetlands disappear, time continues to run out for them. The Iraqi government is determined to rid the country of its vast wetlands. If that happens, the oldest civilization left on earth is likely

Kurdish children cook a small meal in Kurdistan. Kurds make up about 20 percent of the Iraqi population.

language. Most of them live in the mountains of northern Iraq in an area called Kurdistan, a name that means "Land of the Kurds." Kurdistan, which extends into parts of Turkey, Iran, Armenia, and Syria, is more a settlement than a nation, because the Kurdish people have no official country of their own.

The origin of the Kurdish people is somewhat mysterious, even to the Kurds themselves. Some tales trace their roots to mythological figures or ancient Persian kings. A more realistic theory is that the Kurds descended from ancient tribes that moved into northern Iran thousands of years ago and then migrated to Iraq and Turkey. Today, the Kurds are a fiercely proud, independent people. They are loyal to their tribes and to their unique culture. For many decades, they have managed to remain independent, even as various Iraqi governments tried to force them to give up their land.

Most Kurds are Muslims, which means that they practice the Islamic faith. In fact, Islam is the major religion in Iraq, and about 95 percent of Iraqis are Muslims of either the Shia or Sunni sects. About 3 percent of Iraqis are Christians, and a very small number are Jewish. At one time, more than 100,000 Jews lived in Iraq, but today only about 100 are left. Over the years, the Iraqi government has persecuted Jews and driven them out of the country. Most immigrated to Israel. Those who remain in Iraq are too old to make such a move without great hardship.

## Roots in Ancient History

As a nation, Iraq is less than 100 years old, but its Mesopotamian roots trace back for thousands of years. In about 4000 B.C., the Sumerians, who developed one of the most sophisticated civilizations of the ancient world, lived in Mesopotamia and created the earliest known system of writing. Sometime after 2000 B.C., the land became the center of the ancient empires of Babylonia and Assyria. After 1200 B.C., Mesopotamia was conquered and ruled by a succession of Assyrians, Sassanians (Persians), Greeks, and Romans.

Sumerians pressed symbols into wet clay tablets, creating the earliest known system of writing.

In A.D. 635, tribes from Arabia drove out the Romans and took control of Mesopotamia. The Arabs then began to spread their religion, Islam. By the year 651, nearly all of Mesopotamia had been converted to the Islamic faith. Until 1258, the nation was ruled by the Abbasid Dynasty. The Abbasids were Arabic descendants of the prophet Muhammad, whose teachings form the basis of Islam. During this period, the city of Baghdad was founded, and it became a center of knowledge, architecture, literature, and art.

## Baghdad Is Crushed

The Abbasid Dynasty ended when conquerors from Mongolia seized Baghdad. Hordes of soldiers demolished the city and massacred 800,000 people, including the last Abbasid caliph (leader). By the time the Mongols were finished, Baghdad had been reduced to rubble. Centuries' worth of art and architecture lay in ruins. Mackey says that the people of Mesopotamia had always rebuilt what conquerors destroyed—but this time it was different. She explains: "After the Mongols, the broken spirited survivors of the nightmare never began this rebuilding process. . . . Baghdad, the jewel of the Abbasids, lay hopelessly wasted, its exhausted population reduced to a mere 150,000. . . . Only aged broken bricks testified to the forgotten greatness of Mesopotamia."[4]

Over the next centuries, Turkey and Persia fought for control of Mesopotamia. Then, in 1534, a group of Islamic Turks called Ottomans conquered the land. The Ottoman Empire ruled Mesopotamia for more than 300 years.

## Great Britain Takes Control

By the early 1900s, Great Britain had become aware of the vast oil wealth in the Middle East, and the British wanted the rights to this oil. When World War I began in 1914, Great Britain fought with France and

Faisal ibn Husayn (center) was Iraq's first king.

Russia against the Central Powers, which included Germany and Austria-Hungary as well as Turkey, the country of the Ottomans. By 1917, the British had defeated the Ottomans and gained control of Baghdad. When the war ended in 1918, Great Britain controlled all of Mesopotamia.

In 1919, a group of leaders from all over the world gathered in Paris to discuss the future of the Middle East. An agreement called the Covenant of the League of Nations confirmed that Great Britain would rule Mesopotamia. The British would set up a new government for the nation and would eventually give it independence. The British renamed the country Iraq and recognized it as a monarchy. In 1921, Great Britain chose an Arab named Faisal ibn Husayn to be Iraq's first king.

## The Early Years

At first, the Iraqi people resented the new leadership because they saw it as a product of the British government. The new king was also from Arabia, not Iraq, so the people viewed him as a foreigner. Over the next decade, however, the people came to accept Faisal as their head of state. He became known as a stable, credible leader.

In 1924, as a first step toward independence, Faisal and a group of elected Iraqi leaders signed a treaty in which the British promised continued financial support to Iraq. In exchange, Iraq agreed to heed Great Britain's advice on all matters that affected British interests. Within two years, Iraq had elected a parliament, or legislature, to govern its affairs. In 1932, the country became an independent kingdom.

## A Fight for Power

Once Iraq gained its independence, there was intense competition for power. Battles raged between Sunni and Shia Muslim factions, as well as between Kurdish tribes, as the groups tried to secure their places in the new government. The turmoil grew worse in 1933 when Faisal died of heart problems.

Faisal's son, Ghazi, was crowned king after his father's death. Unlike Faisal, Ghazi was not an effective leader. Mackey describes him: "Usually appearing in public in dark sunglasses with a revolver strapped to each hip, he lacked both the [intelligence] and the interest in public affairs necessary for the tough job of being king of Iraq. . . . He spent his time and attention pursuing his own pleasures in urban Baghdad."[5] Ghazi's reign was short. In 1939, he was killed in an automobile accident, and his son, Faisal II, became king. Because the new leader was only three years old, his uncle, Abdul al-Ilah, was appointed to serve in his place until the child was old enough to rule on his own.

## A Time of Turbulence

In 1953, Faisal II turned 18 and began to use his formal powers. Abdul al-Ilah's duties came to an end, but he still had political influence. In 1958, an army led by General Abd al-Karim Kassem took control of

Baghdad. During this military coup, both Faisal II and Abdul al-Ilah were killed. Kassem dissolved the monarchy, proclaimed Iraq a republic, and named himself prime minister. He also declared Islam to be the country's official religion.

The 1960s were turbulent times. Kurdish revolts were common as Kurds fought for their independence. By 1962, they had gained control of much of northern Iraq, although the fighting continued to flare up. With his country in turmoil, Kassem's power and influence weakened. In 1963, a group led by Colonel Abdul Salam Arif overthrew Kassem and assassinated him.

A new government was formed and Arif became Iraq's president. Many key positions in the new regime were held by members of a group called the Ba'ath Party. Arif was not a member of the Ba'aths, though, and less than a year after he became president, he organized a military coup that removed many Ba'aths from power.

President Ahmad Hasan al-Bakr (center) selected Saddam Hussein as his vice president in 1968.

In 1966, Arif was killed in a plane crash, and his brother, Abdul Rahman Mohammad Arif, took over as president. Arif's reign lasted for two years. In 1968, the Iraqi army overthrew the government in a bloodless coup. Ahmad Hasan al-Bakr, a leader of the Ba'ath Party, became Iraq's president. He chose his top security aide, Saddam Hussein—a man known as a brutal enforcer—to be vice president.

# CHAPTER TWO

# Political Turmoil

Once Ahmad Hasan al-Bakr took office, he and Hussein began to take measures to strengthen the new government's power. Iraq had been through decades of turmoil, and the new regime wanted stability. To achieve it, they set up a government that would have complete authority over the people.

During the late 1960s and early 1970s, trouble developed between Iraq and Iran over the boundaries between the two countries. The biggest disagreement was over the Shatt al Arab waterway, which provided access to key ports in both nations. To try to strengthen its defense of the waterway, Iran furnished military aid and supplies to the Kurds. Supported by Iranian funds, Kurdish revolts continued. In 1974, heavy fighting between Iraqi forces and Kurds erupted in northern Iraq.

The Iraqi leaders knew that the Kurds had grown in strength and were a serious threat to the government. So, in 1975, Hussein met with leaders from Iran. Hussein agreed that Iraq would not seek complete control over the Shatt al Arab waterway, and Iran agreed that it would no longer provide military aid to the Kurds. Throughout that year, the Kurds kept

---

Kurdish soldiers stand guard along the border between Iran and Iraq. Tension between the two countries began to develop in the late 1960s over control of a waterway that provided access to key ports.

up ther independence. As promised, Iran did not give them
military When the Iraqi government bombed Kurdish villages
in Iran, ho ensions between the two countries took a turn
for the wors

During hi. s Iraq's leader, al-Bakr's health began to fail and he
started to rely nd more on Hussein to help him run the government. In 1979, resigned. Saddam Hussein became president and
commander-in-c Iraq's armed forces. The country was in his hands.

## War and Destruction

In 1980, Iraq and Iran once again began to quarrel over their borders.
Hussein dissolved the 1975 agreement and announced that the Shatt al
Arab waterway belonged to Iraq alone. Iran protested this declaration,
and hostilities broke out. In September 1980, Hussein ordered Iraqi
troops into Iran. This marked the beginning of a destructive, expensive,
and bloody conflict known as the Iran-Iraq War.

The war dragged on for eight years. It came to an end in 1988,
after the UN negotiated a cease-fire. The violence did not stop inside
Iraq, however. To strike out against the Iraqi government for the way it
continually repressed them, the Kurds had supported Iran in the war.
After the war was over, Hussein vowed revenge. He launched a massive
attack against the Kurds, one of the largest ever waged against a civilian
population. By the time it was over, nearly 1,300 Kurdish villages had
been destroyed. Hama-Amin Hawrami, a Kurdish man who now lives in
the United States, lived in Iraq during the attack. He describes what
happened: "Saddam used all his power and mass destructive weapons,
like poison gases, against Kurdish towns and villages. I lost many
close friends after Saddam's air force hit the town of Halabja. Within

Thousands of Iranian soldiers were killed during the eight-year war between Iraq and Iran.

15 minutes, he killed more than 5,000 people and injured more than 15,000. Members of my family fled to Iran, and for five months I did not have any information about my parents, sisters, and my only brother and his children. Always I was thinking, are they still alive or dead? I do not even want to remember those very dark days."[6]

By the end of 1989, Hussein had become known throughout the world as the Butcher of Baghdad. He received international criticism for the way he treated Iraq's people and particularly for his brutality toward the Kurds. Friction arose between Iraq and many other countries.

In 1990, hostilities began to develop between Iraq and Kuwait. Both countries had originally been part of Mesopotamia, and for many years, Iraqi leaders had claimed that Kuwait was part of Iraq. Hussein shared that viewpoint. In addition, he accused Kuwait of excessive oil production, which reduced the profits that Iraq could earn from its own oil exports. In August 1990, Hussein ordered 120,000 Iraqi troops to invade Kuwait, even though this action was a violation of international law. Once the Iraqi soldiers were in the country, they caused massive destruction and death. Gail Seery, a writer from England who lived in Iraq during the 1970s, explains what happened: "They sent officials with shopping lists [of things to steal], and they literally took what they wanted. They stole planes, trucks, ambulances, computers, medical equipment, horses, zoo animals, boats, cars—you name it, they took it. Then they damaged or destroyed what was left. But far worse than the looting was the widespread torture and murder of Kuwaiti civilians. Iraq still refuses to account for the disappearance of over 600 Kuwaiti civilians, whom the government continued to hold in its jails after the conflict."[7]

The UN Security Council condemned Iraq's invasion of Kuwait and demanded a complete withdrawal. Hussein refused, so the UN passed a series of resolutions that resulted in economic sanctions, or penalties. The sanctions included a full trade embargo, which meant that Iraq could not export and sell any products to other countries, nor could it import any products except for medical supplies and food.

Still, Hussein refused to leave Kuwait, so UN forces—under the direction of the United States—launched the Persian Gulf War. This conflict involved both air and ground attacks against Iraq. Hussein's army struck back. The Iraqis set fire to acres of oil fields and exploded 750 of Kuwait's wells.

---

Iraqi soldiers set fire to Kuwait's oil wells during the Persian Gulf War.

According to a U.S. Department of Defense report, the destruction did not stop there: "Three days later Iraq began pumping Kuwaiti oil into the Persian Gulf, creating an oil slick that covered thousands of square miles."[8] Just six weeks after the war began, Iraqi troops had been defeated and forced out of Kuwait. In February 1991, Hussein agreed to a cease-fire. He said he would comply with UN Security Council resolutions, one of which stated that Iraq would destroy all its weapons of mass destruction, including chemical and biological weapons. If he abided by this agreement, the sanctions would be lifted and Iraq's international trade could return to normal.

Hussein did not keep his promise. Iraq may have been defeated in Kuwait, but Hussein was still in power, and he chose not to follow the Security Council's resolutions. As a result, the UN sanctions stayed in place.

The sanctions produced an economic decline in Iraq that led to a severe shortage of income, high inflation, and drastically reduced wages. Even with donations by international agencies, there was not enough food or medicine to go around, and people could no longer afford to buy what they needed to survive. Aware that the Iraqi people were suffering under the sanctions, the UN offered a program called "oil-for-food," which would allow Iraq to export a certain quantity of oil in exchange for food, medicine, and other essentials.

Hussein repeatedly rejected these offers. He also punished his own people even further in an attempt to force the UN to lift the sanctions. Food—including infant formula—that was sent to Iraq by international relief agencies was stored in government warehouses, rather than distributed to the people. Medicines were confiscated and saved for members of the military to use. Vaccines to protect against diseases such as typhoid, diphtheria, and polio were kept from the people. As a

Weapons inspectors stand at the base of an Iraqi gun. In 1991, Saddam Hussein agreed to destroy all of Iraq's weapons of mass destruction.

result, thousands of Iraqis died from starvation and disease. Even so, Hussein would not accept responsibility for the problems caused by the sanctions. Instead, he publicly blamed the United States and the UN for the Iraqi people's hardships.

For five years, Hussein rejected the UN's oil-for-food proposals. By 1995, the situation in Iraq had gone from bad to desperate. People throughout the country faced starvation, and more than one-fourth of the country's children were malnourished. The death rate had skyrocketed. Finally, in late 1996, Hussein agreed to accept the UN's offer.

The oil-for-food program increased Iraq's income and its supply of food and medicine. Problems remained even after the program was in

# WHAT ARE WEAPONS OF MASS DESTRUCTION?

**All weapons are built to be destructive, but weapons of mass destruction (WMD) are the deadliest weapons on earth.** When they are used, they have the potential to cause enormous devastation over a wide area. The effects of these weapons cannot be predicted or controlled, and WMD can kill thousands of people in an instant. That is why they are also called "weapons of terror."

Nuclear bombs are one of the most dangerous types of WMD. These weapons are so powerful and deadly that their ability to destroy is difficult to imagine. When nuclear bombs explode, they cause waves of intense heat. The temperature is so high, in fact, that objects near the center of the blast can actually be vaporized. This means that heat from the bomb can actually make objects—or living things—disappear entirely. Even people who are not close to a nuclear bomb blast are likely to be

critically burned or to suffer from long-term health problems caused by the bomb's radioactive particles, or fallout.

Chemical and biological weapons are another extremely hazardous form of WMD. They can be used to spread toxic substances called agents. These agents can be spread through the air, through contaminated food and water supplies, or through direct human contact. The most effective way for agents to be spread is by emission into the air, either by an exploding bomb or some type of spray mechanism. In 1995, a terrorist group used chemical weapons in a subway in Tokyo. They spread the poisonous gas with small exploding canisters. Twelve people were killed in the attack and thousands were injured.

Biological weapons spread infectious bacteria or viruses. These weapons can cause diseases such

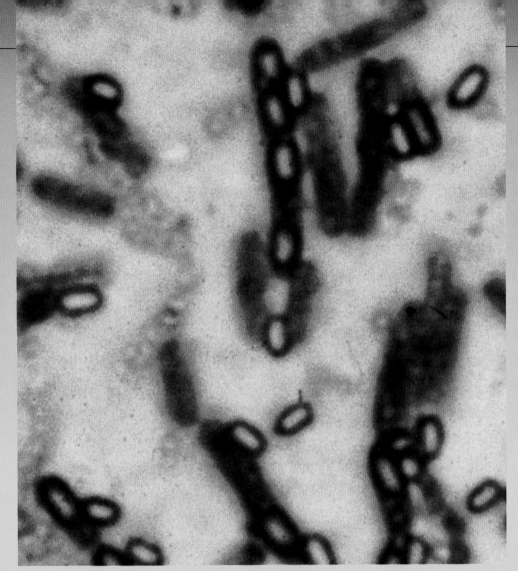

**Weapons of mass destruction, such as missiles that carry anthrax bacterium (pictured), can kill thousands of people very quickly.**

as bubonic plague, malaria, and hepatitis. One of the most feared diseases that can be used as a biological weapon is anthrax, which originated as a disease of hoofed animals, such as cattle, sheep, and horses. Like many bacteria, however, anthrax can be produced in laboratories. When used as a weapon, it is a silent, invisible killer. If it is inhaled, anthrax almost always leads to death.

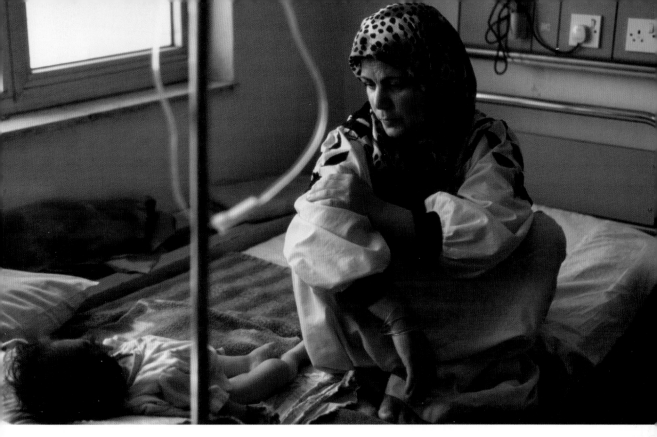

**Above:** A mother watches over her severely malnourished daughter in a hospital. Despite the oil-for-food program, food and medical supplies rarely reach the Iraqi people.

**Left:** Under the oil-for-food program, Iraq can sell oil in exchange for food for its people.

place, however. According to an August 2000 U.S. Department of State report, Hussein continued to "undermine humanitarian efforts" to provide for the Iraqi people: "In northern Iraq, where the UN controls the humanitarian relief programs, child mortality rates are lower than they were before the Gulf War. However, in southern and central Iraq, where the Iraqi government controls the oil-for-food program, mortality rates have doubled. . . . Baghdad has significant resources available to [end] much of Iraq's humanitarian suffering, but Saddam does not spend the money on the Iraqi people."[9]

# CHAPTER THREE

# An Uncertain Future

Throughout the 1990s, hostilities continued to flare up between Iraq and the United States. Hussein refused to live up to the terms of the UN cease-fire agreement. He had agreed to return millions of dollars worth of stolen Kuwaiti property and to account for missing Kuwaitis who had been captured by Iraqi soldiers. He kept neither of these promises. Also, Hussein had agreed to destroy Iraq's weapons of mass destruction and allow UN weapons inspectors to verify this—but he failed to do that. In an effort to force Hussein to abide by the UN agreement, the United States and other coalition countries launched air strikes against Iraqi command centers, missile factories, and airfields.

In 1997, a UN commission learned that Iraq was hiding information about its weapons. That same year, Hussein expelled American UN weapons inspectors from Iraq. Then, in 1998, he halted UN weapons inspections altogether. When the United States and Great Britain threatened further military strikes, Hussein once again agreed to cooperate—and then again failed to keep his promise. Over the next several years, the United States and Great Britain warned Hussein that they would use military force if necessary. In spite of these repeated threats, he continued to defy UN orders.

---

During the 1990s, allied fighter planes patrolled the skies over Iraq.

## Iraq in the Twenty-first Century

Hussein also continued his ruthless treatment of Iraq's people. According to a March 2002 U.S. Department of State report, "Saddam Hussein has ... expanded his violence against women and children; continued his horrific torture and execution of innocent Iraqis; continued to violate the basic human rights of the Iraqi people and has continued to control all sources of information (including killing more than 500 journalists and other opinion leaders in the past decade)."[10]

People throughout the world have often questioned the Iraqi people's seeming tolerance of Hussein's brutality and his complete control over the country. According to Seery, this is a complicated matter: "People have wondered why the Iraqis don't

UN personnel wore protective clothing as they prepared to destroy Iraqi rockets in 1998.

simply stand up and overthrow a regime they know to be bad. The answer is that they truly don't know that life can be different. It is really very similar to children who have been abused—they will accept what has been done to them as 'normal.' Similarly, Iraqis just have no idea what it would be like to be free because they have never truly been free. This makes them guarded. They tend to think that even if Saddam were gone, the next leadership would be just as bad. Or worse."[11]

## An Order to Disarm

In November 2002, the UN Security Council passed an official order for Iraq to disarm. Hussein was given one last chance to disclose and destroy Iraq's weapons of mass destruction. He and Iraqi officials prepared a document that contained more than twelve thousand pages, in which they insisted they had complied with UN requirements. Not everyone believed them, though. Condoleezza Rice, President Bush's national security advisor, said the document was "intended to cloud and confuse the true picture of Iraq's arsenal. It is a reflection of the regime's well-earned reputation for dishonesty."[12] In the following months, UN weapons inspectors were once again allowed back into Iraq, and they found weapons that the Hussein regime had not disclosed. Rice later referred to Iraq's declaration as a "12,200-page lie."[12]

## The Onset of War

On March 17, 2003, President Bush made a public statement that was directed at Saddam Hussein and his sons: Leave Iraq within forty-eight hours or suffer grave consequences. Bush had asked the UN Security Council to support a U.S.-led attack on Iraq if Hussein did not agree to completely disarm. Some countries agreed. Others, such as China, Russia,

The UN Security Council listened to the UN inspectors' report on Iraqi weapons in January 2003.

France, and Germany, stated their strong objection to starting a war. Bush answered by saying: "The United Nations Security Council has not lived up to its responsibilities, so we will rise to ours."[13] Hussein defied Bush's ultimatum, and on March 19, the bombing of Iraq began. An invasion on the ground soon followed. On April 9, Baghdad fell to coalition forces, and within weeks, virtually all of Iraq was under the control of American and British troops. The fate of Hussein was unknown, but there was no doubt that his regime was no longer in power.

# IRAQ'S ROLE IN INTERNATIONAL TERRORISM

**After the September 11, 2001, terrorist attacks on the United States, countries around the world expressed their shock and sympathy.** Among them were many Arab countries—but not Iraq. There is no proof that Iraq was involved in the attacks, and the Iraqi government denies any connection. There is, however, evidence that ties Iraq to other terrorist groups and activities.

Iraq shelters terrorist groups, such as the Mujahedin-e-Khalq Organization (MKO), which has repeatedly used violence against Iran. The MKO has attacked Iranian villages and embassies around the world. Since 1987, the terrorist group has been located in Iraq, and satellite photographs show that a new headquarters has been built. The MKO complex, which is located in the Iraqi city of Falluja, near Baghdad, covers more than two square miles. It

includes buildings, farms, and other facilities. It is large enough to accommodate between 3,000 and 5,000 MKO members.

Another Iraqi facility is Salman Pak, a terrorist training center. Former Iraqi military officers say that training takes place inside a Boeing 707 airplane that lies next to railroad tracks in an area south of Baghdad. According to the officers, terrorists are trained to hijack airplanes and trains and to plant explosives. They also learn how to carry out activities such as sabotage and assassinations. A former Iraqi general who served with Saddam Hussein for many years claimed that Hussein himself supervises the terrorist training.

The Iraqi government has also encouraged terrorism in Israel. For centuries, Jews and Muslims have been enemies because of religious disputes. This has caused hostility between Israel, a Jewish country,

**Saddam Hussein met with Yasser Arafat, the leader of the Palestine Liberation Organization, during a summit in 1989. The Iraqi government supports Palestinian terrorist acts in Israel.**

and Iraq, a Muslim country that supports the Palestinian cause. If Palestinian terrorists die when they carry out a suicide bombing, Hussein pays $25,000 to their families.

Whether the Iraqi government has any connection to al-Qaeda, the terrorist group responsible for the September 11 attacks, is unknown. There is no doubt, however, that Iraq does play a major role in worldwide terrorism.

## The Fate of the People

No one can be sure what the future holds for Iraq. Even the removal of Hussein will not end Iraq's problems immediately. Throughout history, the country's Kurds, Shia Muslims, and Sunni Muslims have competed for power. It is unclear what kind of government can be created to accommodate all of these groups.

In a speech during the winter of 2003, President Bush promised that the United States would not decide who

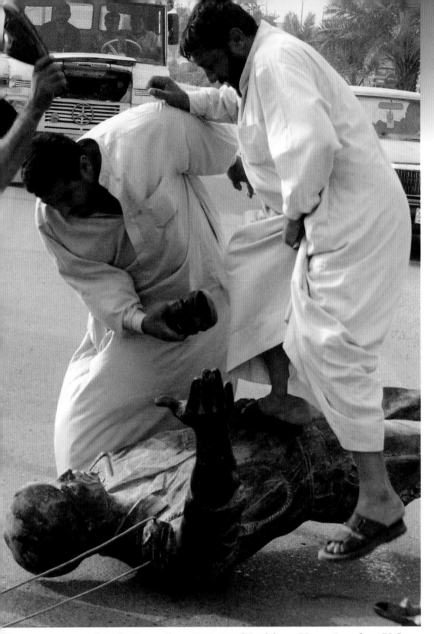
Iraqis trample a statue of Saddam Hussein after U.S. forces rolled into Baghdad on April 9, 2003.

would govern Iraq. That choice, he said, belonged to the Iraqi people. He did say, though, that the U.S. would "ensure that one brutal dictator is not replaced by another" and that rebuilding the country would require "a sustained commitment from many nations."[14]

In the midst of all this turmoil, it is the Iraqi people who suffer the most. They are the ones who must cope with the long-term effects of three wars. They are the ones who have long endured food shortages, poor-quality drinking water, disease, and an inferior health care system. They are the ones who have no idea what tomorrow may bring.

Seery sums up the plight of Iraq's people: "When I lived in Iraq, I got to know many Iraqi people. I found them to be funny, warm, intelligent, and welcoming. They are often painted in an unfavorable light, as if Saddam Hussein is somehow a reflection on them. But he shouldn't be. Because of him, they have been made into something they never wanted to be—aggressors and victims. They have suffered for years, and their lives have been shattered. Like people everywhere, there is something they desperately want and continue to hope for: peace."[15]

The Iraqi people face an uncertain future after years of war and oppression.

# Important Dates

| | |
|---|---|
| **c. 4000 B.C.** | Sumerians live in Mesopotamia; they develop the earliest known system of writing. |
| **c. 2000 B.C.** | Mesopotamia becomes the center of the ancient empires of Babylonia and Assyria. |
| **1200 B.C.–A.D. 635** | Mesopotamia is conquered and ruled by a succession of Assyrians, Sassanians, Greeks, and Romans. |
| **635** | Arab armies drive out Romans and assume control of Mesopotamia; the religion of Islam is introduced. |
| **651** | Nearly all of Mesopotamia is converted to Islam. |
| **750–1258** | Abbasid Dynasty rules Mesopotamia. |
| **1258** | Mongol conquerors seize control of Baghdad. |
| **1534** | Ottoman Empire conquers Mesopotamia; the Ottomans rule for nearly 400 years. |
| **1917** | British invade Baghdad and defeat the Ottomans. |
| **1920** | League of Nations confirms British control over Mesopotamia; British rename the country Iraq and recognize it as a monarchy; British choose Faisal ibn Husayn to be Iraq's first king. |
| **1932** | Iraq is admitted to the League of Nations and becomes an independent kingdom. |
| **1933** | King Faisal I dies; his son, Ghazi, is crowned king. |
| **1939** | Ghazi is killed in an automobile accident; his son, Faisal II, is crowned king. |
| **1953** | Faisal II turns 18 and begins to exercise power. |
| **1958** | Army led by General Abd al-Karim Kassem seizes control of Baghdad; Faisal II is killed; Kassem becomes prime minister and dissolves monarchy; Islam is declared the country's official religion. |
| **1962** | Kurds revolt and gain control over much of northern Iraq. |
| **1963** | Kassem is overthrown and killed. |
| **1968** | Government is overthrown by the army; Ahmad Hasan al-Bakr becomes president; Saddam Hussein becomes vice president. |
| **1975** | Hussein meets with Iranian leaders to settle dispute over Shatt al Arab waterway. |

| 1979 | Al-Bakr resigns; Hussein becomes Iraq's president and commander-in-chief of the army. |
| 1980 | Hussein orders Iraqi troops to invade Iran; Iran-Iraq War begins. |
| 1988 | UN negotiates a cease-fire between Iran and Iraq. Hussein launches massive chemical weapon attack in Kurdistan; thousands of Kurds are killed or injured. |
| 1990 | Iraq invades Kuwait; UN Security Council condemns invasion, orders complete withdrawal; Hussein refuses; UN imposes international sanctions on Iraq. |
| 1991 | UN forces, under the direction of the United States, launch air and land attacks on Iraq, which starts Persian Gulf War. Hussein agrees to a cease-fire; also agrees to disclose and destroy weapons of mass destruction; later refuses to honor the agreement. |
| 1996 | Hussein accepts a UN proposition called the oil-for-food program; sanctions remain in place. |
| 1997 | UN commission determines that Iraq is hiding information on weapons; Hussein expels weapons inspectors from Iraq. |
| 1998 | Hussein halts all weapons inspections. |
| 1998–2002 | Targeted air strikes continue; the UN continues to pressure Hussein to allow weapons inspectors into Iraq. |
| 2003 | U.S. President George W. Bush warns Hussein and his sons to leave Iraq; when they refuse, U.S.-led forces initiate bombing attacks. |

# About the Author

Peggy J. Parks holds a Bachelor of Science degree from Aquinas College in Grand Rapids, Michigan, where she graduated magna cum laude. She is a freelance writer who has written numerous titles for The Gale Group, including the Lucent Books Careers for the 21st Century series, the Blackbirch Press Giants of Science and Nations in Crisis series, and the KidHaven Press Exploring Careers series. She was previously the profile writer for *Grand Rapids: The City That Works*, produced by Towery Publications. Parks lives in Muskegon, Michigan, a town that she says inspires her writing because of its location on the shores of Lake Michigan.

# For More Information

## BOOKS

Leila Merrell Foster, *Iraq.* New York: Childrens Press, 1997. Full-color book includes many facts about Iraq's people, history, and religion.

Susan M. Hassig, *Iraq.* New York: Marshall Cavendish, 1993. Discusses Iraq's geography, history, government, economy, and culture.

John King, *A Family from Iraq.* Austin, TX: Raintree Publishers, 1998. Information about life and customs in Iraq from a family that lives there.

Andrew Lang, ed., *Arabian Nights.* Santa Rosa, CA: Classic Press, 1968. Fifteen selections from the classic folktale, including "Aladdin and the Wonderful Lamp," and "The Seven Voyages of Sinbad the Sailor."

Carol Moss, *Science in Ancient Mesopotamia.* New York: Franklin Watts, 1998. Discusses ancient science among the Babylonians and the Sumerians. Topics include the development of writing, medicine, mathematics, astronomy, and technology.

William Spencer, *Iraq: Old Land, New Nation in Conflict.* Brookfield, CT: Twenty-first Century Books, 2000. Covers Iraq's history, from ancient Mesopotamia to today. Also focuses on the political turbulence and Iraq's problems with international relations.

## PERIODICALS

Mohammad Ali, "No Place to Call Home, Part 1," *New Youth Connections*, April 2000, pp. 16–17. An interesting and frank article by a Kurdish boy about his frightening life in Iraq.

Mohammad Ali, "No Place to Call Home, Part 2," *New Youth Connections*, May/June 2000, pp. 9+. The second part of Ali's story, which focuses on his family's move to America and the challenges of being away from his homeland.

## WEBSITES

**CIA World Factbook—Iraq**
www.cia.gov/cia/publications/factbook/geos/iz.html

**CNN Student News**
http://fyi.cnn.com/fyi/index.html

# Source Quotations

1. Sandra Mackey, *The Reckoning: Iraq and the Legacy of Saddam Hussein.* New York: W.W. Norton, 2002, pp. 11-12.

2. Mackey, *The Reckoning*, p. 10.

3. George W. Bush, "President Bush Addresses the Nation," Iraq: Denial and Deception, March 19, 2003. www.whitehouse.gov.

4. Mackey, *The Reckoning*, pp. 86-87.

5. Mackey, *The Reckoning*, p. 138.

6. Hama-Amin Hawrami, interview with author, September 7, 2002.

7. Gail Seery, interview with author.

8. U.S. Department of Defense, "Iraq and the Gulf War." www.fas.org/irp/gulf/cia/960702/70086_01.htm

9. "Myths and Facts About Iraq," U.S. Department of State International Information Programs, August 2, 2000. http://usinfo.state.gov/regional/nea/iraq/factsheet.htm

10. "Country Reports on Human Rights Practices — Iraq," U.S. Department of State, March 4, 2002. www.state.gov/g/drl/rls/hrrpt/2001/nea/8257.htm

11. Gail Seery, interview with author.

12. Condoleezza Rice, "Why We Know Iraq Is Lying," White House News Releases, January 23, 2003. www.whitehouse.gov/news/releases/2003/01/print/20030123-1.html

13. George W. Bush, "President Says Saddam Hussein Must Leave Iraq Within 48 Hours," President's Address to the Nation, Iraq: Denial and Deception, March 17, 2003. www.whitehouse.gov/news/releases/2003/03/print/20030317-7.html

14. George W. Bush, "President Discusses the Future of Iraq, Iraq: Denial and Deception, February 26, 2003. www.whitehouse.gov/news/releases/2003/02/print/20030226-11.html

15. Gail Seery, interview with author.

# Index